Tough Questions

1 Are you so dull? 3
2 Who can forgive sins? 7
3 Who do you say I am? 11
4 What must I do? 15
5 My God, my God, why? 19
   Tough conclusions 24

Tough Questions
© Matthias Media 1994

Matthias Media
(St Matthias Press Ltd ACN 067 558 365)
PO Box 225
Kingsford NSW 2032
Australia
Telephone: (02) 9663 1478; international: +61-2-9663-1478
Facsimile: (02) 9663 3265; international: +61-2-9663-3265
Email: info@matthiasmedia.com.au
Internet: www.matthiasmedia.com.au

Matthias Media (USA)
Telephone: 724 964 8152; international: +1-724-964-8152
Facsimile: 724 964 8166; international: +1-724-964-8166
Email: sales@matthiasmedia.com
Internet: www.matthiasmedia.com

Scripture quotations are taken from the HOLY BIBLE, NEW INTERNATIONAL VERSION. Copyright © 1973, 1978, 1984 by International Bible Society. Used by permission.

ISBN 978 1 875245 33 8

All rights reserved. Except as may be permitted by the Copyright Act, no part of this publication may be reproduced in any form or by any means without prior permission from the publisher.

Typesetting and cover design by Lankshear Design Pty Ltd.

1

Are you so dull?

¹The Pharisees and some of the teachers of the law who had come from Jerusalem gathered round Jesus and ²saw some of his disciples eating food with hands that were "unclean", that is, unwashed. ³(The Pharisees and all the Jews do not eat unless they give their hands a ceremonial washing, holding to the tradition of the elders. ⁴When they come from the market-place they do not eat unless they wash. And they observe many other traditions, such as the washing of cups, pitchers and kettles.)

⁵So the Pharisees and teachers of the law asked Jesus, "Why don't your disciples live according to the tradition of the elders instead of eating their food with 'unclean' hands?"

⁶He replied, "Isaiah was right when he prophesied about you hypocrites; as it is written:

"These people honour me with their lips, but their hearts are far from me.
⁷*They worship me in vain: their teachings are but rules taught by men."*

⁸You have let go of the commands of God and are holding on to the traditions of men."

⁹And he said to them: "You have a fine way of setting aside the commands of God in order to observe your own traditions! ¹⁰For Moses said, 'Honour your father and your mother,' and,'Anyone who curses his father or mother must be put to death.' ¹¹But you say that if a man says to his father or mother: 'Whatever help you might otherwise have received from me is Corban' (that is, a gift devoted to God), ¹²then you no longer let him do anything for his father or mother. ¹³Thus you nullify the word of God by your tradition that you have handed down. And you do many things like that."

¹⁴Again Jesus called the crowd to him and said, "Listen to me, everyone, and understand this. ¹⁵Nothing outside a man can make him 'unclean' by going into him. Rather, it is what comes out of a man that makes him 'unclean'."

¹⁷After he had left the crowd and entered the house, his disciples asked him about this parable. ¹⁸**"Are you so dull?"** he asked. "Don't you see that nothing that enters a man from the outside can make him 'unclean'? ¹⁹For it doesn't go into his heart but into his stomach, and then out of his body." (In saying this, Jesus declared all foods "clean".)

^{20}He went on: "What comes out of a man is what makes him 'unclean'. ^{21}For from within, out of men's hearts, come evil thoughts, sexual immorality, theft, murder, adultery, ^{22}greed, malice, deceit, lewdness, envy, slander, arrogance and folly. ^{23}All these evils come from inside and make a man 'unclean'."

MARK 7:1-23

Note: The numbered questions can be answered directly from the Bible passage. The 'Think it Through' questions help you to think further about what it means.

1   What did the Jewish leaders object to? (verses 1-5)

2   How did the Jewish leaders try to make themselves acceptable to God (that is, 'clean')? (verses 1-5)

THINK IT THROUGH

How do most people try to make themselves acceptable to God?

What food regulations are followed by religious people today?

3 Why does Jesus call the Jewish leaders hypocrites? (verses 6-8)

4 What example does Jesus give of their hypocrisy? (verses 9-13)

5 What does Jesus say about religious traditions? (verses 9-13)

THINK IT THROUGH

What are some of the religious traditions of our society?

How do people today use religion to avoid God?

6   Why were the disciples dull? (verse 18)

7   You might have heard people say, "I'm not perfect. I've got my faults. But I'm basically good at heart." What do you think Jesus would say to them? (verses 14-23)

THINK IT THROUGH

How accurate is Jesus' assessment of human nature?

Why can't religious rituals make us acceptable to God?

What hope do we have of being accepted by God?

ns?

2

Who can forgive sins?

¹A few days later, when Jesus again entered Capernaum, the people heard that he had come home. ²So many gathered that there was no room left, not even outside the door, and he preached the word to them. ³Some men came, bringing to him a paralytic, carried by four of them. ⁴Since they could not get him to Jesus because of the crowd, they made an opening in the roof above Jesus and, after digging through it, lowered the mat the paralysed man was lying on. ⁵When Jesus saw their faith, he said to the paralytic, "Son, your sins are forgiven."

⁶Now some teachers of the law were sitting there, thinking to themselves, ⁷"Why does this fellow talk like that? He's blaspheming! **Who can forgive sins but God alone?**"

⁸Immediately Jesus knew in his spirit that this was what they were thinking in their hearts, and he said to them, "Why are you thinking these things? ⁹Which is easier: to say to the paralytic, 'Your sins are forgiven,' or to say, 'Get up, take your mat and walk'? ¹⁰But that you may know that the Son of Man has authority on earth to forgive sins..." He said to the paralytic, ¹¹"I tell you, get up, take your mat and go home." ¹²He got up, took his mat and walked out in full view of them all. This amazed everyone and they praised God, saying, "We have never seen anything like this!"

MARK 2:1-12

1   What is strange about Jesus' statement in verse 5?

2   What is meant by "sins"? (verses 5, 7, 10)

3   Why did Jesus declare this man forgiven?

_____

_____

THINK IT THROUGH

What do people feel guilty about?

_____

_____

_____

_____

Are these guilty feelings different from what Jesus means by "sin"? How?

_____

_____

_____

_____

How do people try to relieve their guilty feelings?

_____

_____

_____

_____

How does Jesus deal with the problem of sin?

_____

_____

_____

---

4   What did the teachers of the law conclude? (verses 6-7)

_____

_____

_____

5   What is Jesus claiming about himself? (verses 8-12)

    _____
    _____
    _____

6   How did he back up his claims?

    _____
    _____

THINK IT THROUGH

Look at the question Jesus asks in verse 9. How do you think these different people would answer it?

   The teachers of the law:
   _____
   _____

   Jesus:
   _____
   _____

   Someone today:
   _____
   _____

Which do you think is easier?
_____
_____

If Jesus was right about himself, how does it affect us?
_____
_____
_____

3

Who do you say I am?

²⁷Jesus and his disciples went on to the villages around Caesarea Philippi. On the way he asked them, "Who do people say I am?"

²⁸They replied, "Some say John the Baptist; others say Elijah; and still others, one of the prophets."

²⁹"But what about you?" he asked. **"Who do you say I am?"**

Peter answered, "You are the Christ."

³⁰Jesus warned them not to tell anyone about him.

31He then began to teach them that the Son of Man must suffer many things and be rejected by the elders, chief priests and teachers of the law, and that he must be killed and after three days rise again. ³²He spoke plainly about this, and Peter took him aside and began to rebuke him.

³³But when Jesus turned and looked at his disciples, he rebuked Peter. "Get behind me, Satan!" he said, "You do not have in mind the things of God, but the things of men."

³⁴Then he called the crowd to him along with his disciples and said: "If anyone would come after me, he must deny himself and take up his cross and follow me. ³⁵For whoever wants to save his life will lose it, but whoever loses his life for me and for the gospel will save it. ³⁶What good is it for a man to gain the whole world, yet forfeit his soul? ³⁷Or what can a man give in exchange for his soul? ³⁸If anyone is ashamed of me and my words in this adulterous and sinful generation, the Son of Man will be ashamed of him when he comes in his Father's glory with the holy angels."

MARK 8:27-38

1 What did Jesus' contemporaries think of him? (verses 27-28)

_____

_____

_____

2   What is surprising about Jesus' attitude to himself? (verses 29-30)

THINK IT THROUGH

What opinions do our contemporaries hold about Jesus?

How do they arrive at these opinions?

3   What does Jesus say about his future? (verses 31-38)

4   What was Peter's mistake? (verses 32-33)

5   Who does Jesus think he is?

THINK IT THROUGH

How could we make Peter's mistake?

Who do you think Jesus was?

What is the basis of your opinion?

6   What does Jesus say about people's destiny? (verses 34-38)

THINK IT THROUGH

In today's world, what do people live for?

If Jesus' claims about himself are true, how should you live?

_____
_____
_____
_____

4

What must I do?

¹⁷As Jesus started on his way, a man ran up to him and fell on his knees before him. "Good teacher," he asked, "**what must I do** to inherit eternal life?"

¹⁸"Why do you call me good?" Jesus answered. "No-one is good—except God alone. ¹⁹You know the commandments: 'Do not murder, do not commit adultery, do not steal, do not give false testimony, do not defraud, honour your father and mother.'"

²⁰"Teacher," he declared, "all these I have kept since I was a boy."

²¹Jesus looked at him and loved him. "One thing you lack," he said. "Go, sell everything you have and give to the poor, and you will have treasure in heaven. Then come, follow me."

²²At this the man's face fell. He went away very sad, because he had great wealth.

²³Jesus looked around and said to his disciples, "How hard it is for the rich to enter the kingdom of God!"

²⁴The disciples were amazed at his words. But Jesus said again, "Children, how hard it is to enter the kingdom of God! ²⁵It is easier for a camel to go through the eye of a needle than for a rich man to enter the kingdom of God."

²⁶The disciples were even more amazed, and said to each other, "Who then can be saved?"

²⁷Jesus looked at them and said, "With man this is impossible, but not with God: all things are possible with God."

²⁸Peter said to him "We have left everything to follow you!"

²⁹"I tell you the truth," Jesus replied, "no-one who has left home or brothers or sisters or mother or father or children or fields for me and the gospel ³⁰will fail to receive a hundred times as much in this present age (homes, brothers, sisters, mothers, children and fields—and with them, persecutions) and in the age to come, eternal life. But many who are first will be last, and the last first."

MARK 10:17-31

1. How would you describe the rich man? (verses 17-20)

THINK IT THROUGH

How was the rich man trying to gain eternal life?

Why did the attempt fail?

How do people today try to gain eternal life?

---

2. Many people regard wealth as a sign of God's blessing. What does Jesus say?

3. How does Jesus answer the rich man's question? (verses 17-21)

THINK IT THROUGH

How does Jesus' value system differ from that of our community?

Why is it hard for rich people to enter the kingdom of God? (verse 23)

What does Jesus reveal about his view of himself?

4 What does it mean to "follow" Jesus? (verses 21, 28, 29)

5 What does Jesus promise his followers? (verses 29-31)

THINK IT THROUGH

What is attractive about following Jesus?

What might stop you following Jesus?

5

My God, my God, why?

⁵³They took Jesus to the high priest, and all the chief priests, elders and teachers of the law came together. ⁵⁴Peter followed him at a distance, right into the courtyard of the high priest. There he sat with the guards and warmed himself at the fire.

⁵⁵The chief priests and the whole Sanhedrin were looking for evidence against Jesus so that they could put him to death, but they did not find any. ⁵⁶Many testified falsely against him, but their statements did not agree.

⁵⁷Then some stood up and gave this false testimony against him: ⁵⁸"We heard him say, 'I will destroy this man-made temple and in three days will build another, not made by man.'" ⁵⁹Yet even then their testimony did not agree.

⁶⁰Then the high priest stood up before them and asked Jesus, "Are you not going to answer? What is this testimony that these men are bringing against you?" ⁶¹But Jesus remained silent and gave no answer.

Again the high priest asked him, "Are you the Christ, the Son of the Blessed One?"

⁶²"I am," said Jesus. "and you will see the Son of Man sitting at the right hand of the Mighty One and coming on the clouds of heaven."

⁶³The high priest tore his clothes. "Why do we need any more witnesses?" he asked. ⁶⁴"You have heard the blasphemy. What do you think?"

They all condemned him as worthy of death. ⁶⁵Then some began to spit at him; they blindfolded him, struck him with their fists, and said, "Prophesy!" And the guards took him and beat him.

MARK 14:53-65

¹Very early in the morning, the chief priests, with the elders, the teachers of the law and the whole Sanhedrin, reached a decision. They bound Jesus, led him away and turned him over to Pilate.

²"Are you the king of the Jews?" asked Pilate.

"Yes, it is as you say," Jesus replied.

³The chief priests accused him of many things. ⁴So again Pilate asked him,

"Aren't you going to answer? See how many things they are accusing you of."

⁵But Jesus still made no reply, and Pilate was amazed.

⁶Now it was the custom at the Feast to release a prisoner whom the people requested. ⁷A man called Barabbas was in prison with the insurrectionists who had committed murder in the uprising. ⁸The crowd came up and asked Pilate to do for them what he usually did.

⁹"Do you want me to release to you the king of the Jews?" asked Pilate, ¹⁰knowing it was out of envy that the chief priests had handed Jesus over to him. ¹¹But the chief priests stirred up the crowd to have Pilate release Barabbas instead.

¹²"What shall I do, then, with the one you call the king of the Jews?" Pilate asked them.

¹³"Crucify him!" they shouted.

¹⁴"Why? What crime has he committed?" asked Pilate.

But they shouted all the louder, "Crucify him!"

¹⁵Wanting to satisfy the crowd, Pilate released Barabbas to them. He had Jesus flogged, and handed him over to be crucified.

¹⁶The soldiers led Jesus away into the palace (that is, the Praetorium) and called together the whole company of soldiers. ¹⁷They put a purple robe on him, then twisted together a crown of thorns and set it on him. ¹⁸And they began to call out to him, "Hail, king of the Jews!" ¹⁹Again and again they struck him on the head with a staff and spat on him. Falling on their knees, they paid homage to him. ²⁰And when they had mocked him, they took off the purple robe and put his own clothes on him. They led him out to crucify him.

²¹A certain man from Cyrene, Simon, the father of Alexander and Rufus, was passing by on his way in from the country, and they forced him to carry the cross. ²²They brought Jesus to the place called Golgotha (which means The Place of the Skull). ²³Then they offered him wine mixed with myrrh, but he did not take it. ²⁴And they crucified him. Dividing up his clothes, they cast lots to see what each would get.

²⁵It was the third hour when they crucified him. ²⁶The written notice of the charge against him read: THE KING OF THE JEWS. ²⁷They crucified two robbers with him, one on his right and one on his left. ²⁹Those who passed by hurled insults at him, shaking their heads and saying, "So! You who are going to destroy the temple and build it in three days, ³⁰come down from the cross and save yourself!"

³¹In the same way the chief priests and the teachers of the law mocked him among themselves. "He saved others," they said, "but he can't save himself! ³²Let this Christ, this King of Israel, come down now from the cross, that we may see and believe." Those crucified with him also heaped insults on him.

³³At the sixth hour darkness came over the whole land until the ninth hour.

[34] And at the ninth hour Jesus cried out in a loud voice, "Eloi, Eloi, lama sabachthani?"—which means, '**My God, my God, why** have you forsaken me?'

[35] When some of those standing near heard this, they said, "Listen, he's calling Elijah."

[36] One man ran, filled a sponge with wine vinegar, put it on a stick, and offered it to Jesus to drink. "Now leave him alone. Let's see if Elijah comes to take him down," he said.

[37] With a loud cry, Jesus breathed his last.

[38] The curtain of the temple was torn in two from top to bottom. [39] And when the centurion, who stood there in front of Jesus, heard his cry and saw how he died, he said, "Surely this man was the Son of God!"

[40] Some women were watching from a distance. Among them were Mary Magdalene, Mary the mother of James the younger and of Joses, and Salome. [41] In Galilee these women had followed him and cared for his needs. Many other women who had come up with him to Jerusalem were also there.

MARK 15:1-41

1. Why did the Jewish leaders want Jesus dead?

   _____
   _____

2. Why did Pilate want Jesus dead?

   _____
   _____

3. Who did Jesus think he was?

   _____
   _____

THINK IT THROUGH

Were the charges against Jesus true? (compare Mark 8:29 in study 3)

_____
_____
_____
_____

> *Why didn't Jesus answer his accusers? (compare Mark 8:31-32 in study 3)*

4. How did Jesus understand his own death? (15:34; compare Mark 10:45—"For even the Son of Man did not come to the be served, but to serve, and to give his life as a ransom for many.")

THINK IT THROUGH

In what sense did Jesus give his life as a 'ransom'?

Why would God forsake Jesus?

Why was the temple curtain torn in two? (15:38)

5. What attitude did these people have to Jesus' execution?
   The soldiers (15:16-20)

The Jewish leaders (15:31-32)

The crowd (15:29-30, 35-36)

The centurion (15:38-39)

THINK IT THROUGH

Who killed Jesus?

Does Jesus save others? (15:31)

Does Jesus save himself? (15:31)

What is your attitude to the execution of Jesus?

Tough conclusions

From these tough questions in Mark's Gospel, what have you concluded about:

1 Who Jesus is?

___

2 Why Jesus died?

___

3 How you can be friends with God?

___